Table of Contents

"All right," said the Cheshire Cat; and this time it vanished quite slowly, beginning with the end of the tail, and ending with the grin, which remained some time after the rest of it had gone.

—Lewis Carroll, *Alice's Adventures in Wonderland*

CHAPTER 1

AMELIA AND THE GAS GAUGE

They called her Lady Lindy, after Charles Lindbergh, the most famous male pilot of the day. She had a broad, gap-toothed grin that made her large eyes dance behind her flyboy goggles. And she wasn't a half-bad pilot—for a dame, that is. Yeah, she held her own, all right. Made the 2,400-mile run from Hawaii to California. Crossed the Atlantic all alone. Gulf of Mexico too. Everybody knew her.

By 1937 Amelia Earhart was a world-famous pilot. She had flown across the Atlantic Ocean twice and had completed a 2,400-mile solo flight across the Pacific Ocean.

She was Amelia Earhart, and in the 1930s, was the slickest thing in the skies. So it was downright weird that she just disappeared like that. They said that her last message came through at quarter to nine in the morning, July 3, 1937. I was 10 at the time. "We are on the line of position 157–337....We are running north and south." That's what she said. And that's all she said.

Well, they searched, of course. Ten ships and 65 planes were out there over the Pacific looking for Lady Lindy. Didn't find a thing. Not one scrap. It was like the clouds swallowed her up. If she'd crashed, there would have been wreckage, don't you think? If she'd been in trouble, she would have radioed a Mayday, right? Poor kid. I wonder whatever happened to her.

It has been almost 70 years since Amelia Earhart and her navigator, Frederick Noonan, disappeared somewhere over the Pacific Ocean. But the mystery of what became of them still intrigues us. Earhart's plan was to circle the globe at the equator—a 29,000-mile trip that no one had ever before attempted.

THE BIG BLUE

The Pacific Ocean is the world's largest, deepest, and oldest ocean. It's also the world's largest geographical feature, covering one-third of the surface of the earth. The ocean's 70 million square miles are dotted with 30,000 islands, most grouped together as the Pacific Islands, or Oceania. Some Pacific Islands are no larger than a suburban backyard. In fact, if you subtracted the mass of the largest islands—Hawaii, New Guinea, and New Zealand—the remaining thousands put together would be no bigger than the state of Indiana.

The Pacific has vast stretches of open ocean and uninhabited islands.

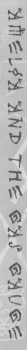

She took off heading east from Oakland, California, flying a Lockheed 10-E Electra fitted with extra large fuel tanks and radio navigation gear. Her first stop was Miami, Florida. From there she flew out over the Caribbean Sea and on to South America, Africa, India, Burma, and Australia.

Despite insomnia, nausea, and severe stomach cramps, Earhart pushed on, logging 22,000 miles before she set her plane down on a grassy landing strip in Lae, New Guinea, in the South Pacific Ocean. Both Earhart and Noonan were showing signs of exhaustion, and the most dangerous part of the trip lay ahead of them.

Only 7,000 miles of their journey back to California remained. But it was 7,000 miles of featureless ocean. Earhart's navigational target was a tiny atoll (a ring-shaped coral island) 1,650 miles southwest of Honolulu, Hawaii. Howland Island, with no permanent inhabitants, is a

In San Juan, Puerto Rico, Earhart and Noonan packed their plane for the transatlantic leg of their journey.

GUTS AND LUCK

In the early days of aviation, a pilot needed guts and a lot of luck. Before electronic instruments, flying was literally hit or miss. Pilots relied on land features to guide them to their destinations. They followed railroad tracks, light beacons, roads, and rivers. As they drew closer to their target, they looked for specific markers, such as a church steeple or a design on a rooftop. But if the weather turned bad and visibility dropped, a pilot could easily become disoriented. Without instruments and unable to see the horizon line, a pilot had no way of knowing whether he or she was "flying right." This inability to tell up from down was the main reason so many planes crashed.

Earhart and Noonan had compasses and some other instruments. But they were still depending on land features to help them reach Hawaii. And over the vast South Pacific, those features were few and far between.

mile-and-a-half-long speck and a challenge to find even with modern, sophisticated equipment. For Earhart, Howland was just barely within range.

>> Final Flight

Earhart and Noonan took off from Lae on the morning of July 2. The U.S. Coast Guard cutter *Itasca* waited offshore of Howland in case Earhart needed help locating the island. Earhart estimated that she and Noonan would arrive at Howland in 24 hours.

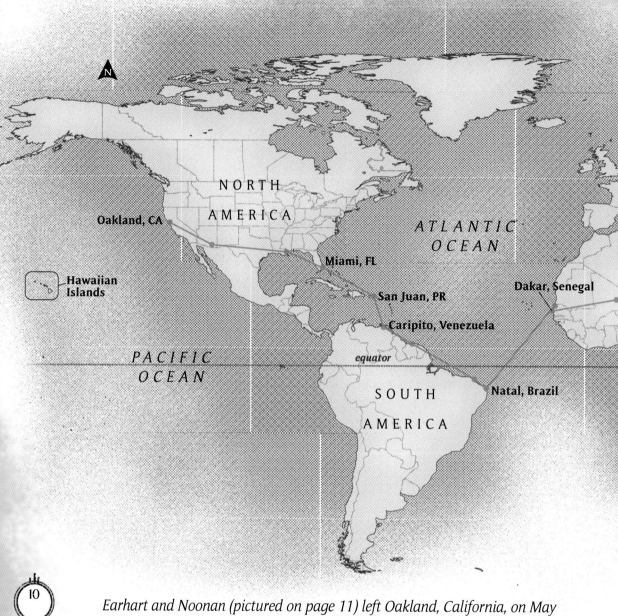

NORTH
AMERICA

ATLANTIC
OCEAN

Oakland, CA

Hawaiian
Islands

Miami, FL

San Juan, PR

Dakar, Senegal

Caripito, Venezuela

PACIFIC
OCEAN

equator

SOUTH
AMERICA

Natal, Brazil

10

Earhart and Noonan (pictured on page 11) left Oakland, California, on May 21, 1937. They headed south toward the equator, tracing a route across Florida, Puerto Rico, and northern South America. From Natal, Brazil, they crossed over to Senegal, Africa, and continued across the continent. From Africa, Earhart and Noonan flew over the Arabian Sea to Pakistan, India, Southeast Asia, Indonesia, and Australia. The last leg of their journey was the

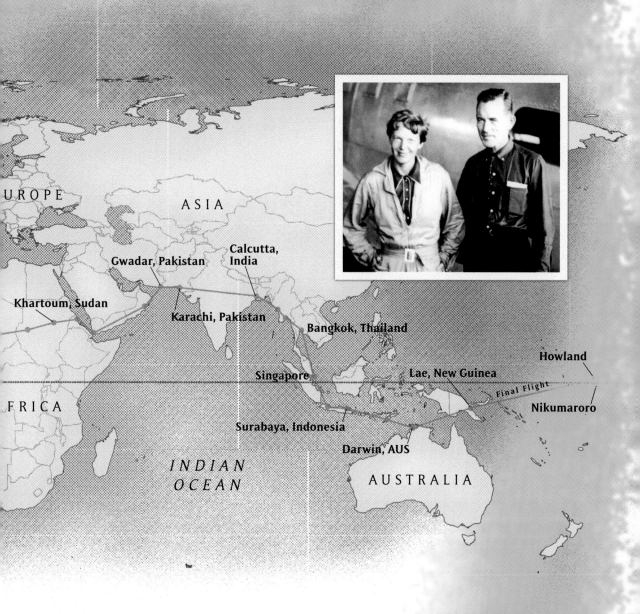

most difficult. *After Lae, New Guinea, Earhart and Noonan faced 2,556 miles of featureless Pacific before reaching their next target, tiny Howland Island, near Honolulu, Hawaii. Noonan prepared to navigate half the journey in the dark, since they'd be flying at night. Meanwhile, near Howland Island, U.S navy ships lit all their lights, to serve as markers. The* Itasca *also sent up a plume of black smoke, visible from the plane's altitude.*

Twenty hours into the flight, Earhart established radio contact with *Itasca.* A little while later, she radioed back to ask for a compass heading. *Itasca* heard nothing for about an hour, and then, "We must be on you, *Itasca,* but cannot see you. Gas is running low. We have been unable to reach you by radio."

The *Itasca* operator responded, but he did not receive an acknowledgment. After about 15 minutes, Earhart again radioed to ask for a heading. The *Itasca* responded but then heard nothing further until 8:44 A.M., local time. It turned out to be Earhart's last transmission. She was less than 2,000 nautical miles from Hawaii.

What happened to Amelia Earhart?

The newspaper headline reads:

Liberty Scout Wins 2d Delaware

THE EVENING SUN | **Sports 6 Star** | SATURDAY SPECIAL

Budge Wins 3 Titles, Wimbledon Record

RADIO MEN HEAR EARHART'S VOICE FAINTLY ASKING FOR AID.

The *Baltimore Evening Sun* reported that Earhart may have radioed for help after the plane disappeared. Such reports helped fuel the hope that she and Noonan would be found alive.

Some suggested that she had actually been on a secret mission for the government. Instead of heading east when she left New Guinea, she flew north toward the Caroline Islands (modern Palau and Micronesia). As Earhart and Noonan approached Saipan, one of the Mariana Islands, the Electra was shot down by Japanese soldiers patrolling the islands. Earhart and Noonan were taken prisoner and executed. Others thought she and Noonan had landed on a romantic tropical isle and were frolicking on the warm sand, glad to be rid of the pressures of civilized life. And once people started sighting UFOs, they naturally blamed the grabby little aliens for Earhart's disappearance. The most likely scenario, though, had Earhart running out of fuel and crashing into the Pacific. But despite an extensive search that began within hours of Earhart's last communication, neither bodies nor wreckage were ever found.

>> Gone without a Trace?

The years pass. It's now four decades later, and Ric Gillespie of the International Group for Historic Aircraft Recovery (TIGHAR) is working on his own rather intriguing theory. Earhart and Noonan were certainly low on fuel, he says, but they had just enough to set their plane down on a coral reef close to the South Pacific island of Nikumaroro. They made their way to the uninhabited atoll, where they eventually died of starvation and exposure.

Gillespie has made four trips to Nikumaroro in his search for clues, but whatever he has found so far is less than convincing. He has fragments of a woman's shoe and a sheet of aluminum from a plane.

However, the rivet pattern on the aluminum does not match the Electra's. A couple of years after Earhart's disappearance, explorers

Earhart is shown testing her plane's life raft before packing it on board. If the plane went down in the ocean, Earhart and Noonan could have escaped the wreckage on the raft.

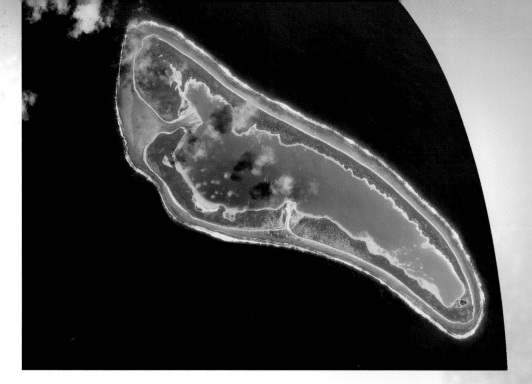

Nikumaroro is an atoll. Even if Earhart and Noonan reached Nikumaroro, they had no fresh water or food and no shelter from the blazing sun.

supposedly discovered bones on the island. But the bones are long gone. Still, Gillespie is confident he is on the right track.

Elgen Long begs to differ. Long has spent more than two decades piecing together Earhart's flight path and believes Earhart's plane ran out of fuel and plunged into the Pacific. And it is resting, he says, 35 miles west-northwest of Howland Island, in a cold, watery grave, 17,000 feet down.

An eerie, bleached skeleton of Amelia would not, however, be sitting in the flooded cockpit. The salty Pacific Ocean would have long ago dissolved her mortal remains. But the Electra's aluminum fuselage would likely be resting on the bottom, parked in its final hangar, patiently waiting for the tourists to at last arrive.

CHAPTER 2

CHRIS AND
THE TRIANGLE

If you ask me, I don't think the admiral knew where he was going half the time. I was on the Pinta *with 26 other men when we sailed from Palos on the Spanish coast to what I found out later were the Canary Islands, off the coast of West Africa. The admiral thought we'd reached China. See what I mean?*

Well, after that, we headed west. We caught the trade winds and made pretty good progress, averaging about 140 miles a day. Of course, there wasn't an awful lot to see because by then we were on open ocean, bound for either glory or disaster—take your pick.

We were somewhere in the North Atlantic, I think, when we started to come into some really thick seaweed, and let me tell you, it was nasty. But the admiral—if you can believe it—was practically doing a jig on the deck. "We're almost there, boys!" he cried. "Seaweed's a sign that we're close to land." But then the wind died down, and it didn't look like it was going to rain any time soon, and there we sat, not exactly confident.

Even though the admiral kept telling us not to worry, any fool could see we were in trouble. The current was carrying us in a weird clockwise direction, and the ship's compass had started to go haywire. When we complained to the admiral, he just waved us off. "A compass never points to true north," he said. "It's always off a little." Oh, sure, we all thought, rolling our eyes. And Queen Isabella is really a mermaid.

The *Pinta*, the *Niña*, and the *Santa Maria (facing page)* first set sail across the Atlantic Ocean from Spain in 1492. The ships were guided by Christopher Columbus *(left)*, an Italian navigator who was looking for a route to Asia.

I'll tell you what I think. I think good old Admiral Where-in-the-world-am-I? had blundered into some kind of haunted sea—not that it bothered him any. He's talking about coming back here again next year. You'd think I'd be scared to sail with him, but I'm not. Like I said, the guy has a lousy sense of direction. We'll probably wind up in Egypt.

Sailing west from the Canary Islands, Columbus could hardly avoid the region that would one day be called the Sargasso Sea. It is a vast, slow-flowing field of brown gulfweed, roughly the size of the continental United States. Here, the weather is almost diabolically calm, and the surrounding currents create a lazy whirlpool, like soup just coming to a boil. It is hot, dry, and windless, a place where a ship may

THE HORSE LATITUDES

Sailing with the wind was tricky and dangerous, an adventure that could scare the pants off you as well as stir your spirit. As long as a steady wind filled the sails, a ship made good progress. But when the wind died, the sea could hold a ship hostage for days on end as food and water slowly dwindled away.

Sailors quickly learned to beware of two weather belts that girdle the earth near the latitudes of 30°N and 30°S. The subtropic oceans under these weather belts are often very calm, with light winds. The belts became known as the horse latitudes because, according to legend, Spanish sailors transporting horses to the New World often had to resort to throwing the horses overboard to conserve water.

Stories of hideous sea creatures abounded in European exploration. Sailors were nervous about traveling unknown waters, and large, unfamiliar fish easily became "monsters."

drift for days, her sails as limp as bedsheets, her hull creaking for want of a rescuing breeze.

To Columbus's crew, the Sargasso Sea was unfamiliar and frightening. But while Columbus himself was carefully recording the facts in his ship's log, his men were doing just the opposite. Fueled by superstition and an I-bet-you-can't-top-this mentality, the sailors cooked up quite a tasty tale for the folks back home. By the time they reached Portugal, the seaweed had become a sinister life-form that crawled up and over the rails and lashed sailors to the masts. Instead of dolphins and tuna, horrible sea serpents rose from the darkened depths. Fire poured from the sky, and a bubbling whirlpool threatened to spin the three square-riggers to a watery death. Compass needles turned crazily in the magnetic vacuum, and . . .

Hey, wait a minute! This sounds a lot like a prototype for the Bermuda Triangle!

And indeed, that is exactly what it is. Five centuries later, there are aliens instead of sea serpents and a vortex instead of a whirlpool. The seaweed is no longer mentioned, and when fire rains from the sky, it's called a meteor shower. But the magnetic vacuum is still there, sucking

The Bermuda Triangle originally traced its shape from Florida to Puerto Rico to Bermuda. But it expanded to include much of the U.S. East Coast and the central Atlantic.

up sailing ships, fishing boats, Beechcraft planes, DC-3s, and fighter jets with equal relish.

The first modern Bermuda Triangle stretched from the tip of Florida to Bermuda to Puerto Rico. But when Flight 19 was lost in 1945 just north of the Triangle, a Bermuda Square had to be drawn to include it. Then a Bermuda Trapezoid was needed for the disappearance of the *Star Tiger* in 1948. The latest Bermuda "Triangle" is a great big five-sided figure that takes in the entire East Coast of the United States, all the way down to South America, and east to the Azores. The Azores were added to include the *Mary Celeste,* one of the glue globs that keeps the myth of the Bermuda Triangle stuck together.

FLIGHT 19

Almost every Bermuda Triangle book opens with the "mystery" of Flight 19. Five navy bomber planes flying in formation suddenly vanished on a routine training mission in 1945. How could five experienced pilots just disappear? Well, the pilots were actually trainees following a flight leader whose compass had failed. The sea was rough, and fuel was running low. Add it up, and you get a tragic, but not very mysterious, disappearance.

>> The Mystery of the *Mary Celeste*

The story of the *Mary Celeste* is a true mystery. It is, in fact, one of a handful of disappearances that remain unexplained. (Nearly all the others have been attributed to bad weather, engine or structural failure, pilot error or, in one case, a possible hijacking.)

The *Mary Celeste* had sailed for Genoa, Italy, from New York City in November 1872. Her captain was Benjamin Briggs, and he took with him his wife, young daughter, and a crew of eight. On December 4, 1872, another ship, the *Dei Gratia,* found the *Mary Celeste* abandoned and drifting, nearly 600 miles west of Gibraltar.

Nothing seemed amiss on board the two-masted ship. The cargo was intact, and the galley was ship-shape, with six months' worth of untouched provisions.

The *Mary Celeste* was a type of two-masted sailing ship called a half-brigantine. Half-brigs were often used as merchant ships, carrying cargo from a seller to a buyer.

The sails were torn but still quite serviceable. The ship's log lay where the captain had left it, his final entry noting that they had passed the Azores on November 24. Only two things were missing (aside from the 11 people, of course): the ship's official papers and the lifeboat.

At first, the solution to the mystery seems ridiculously obvious. Everybody piled into the lifeboat and rowed away. But why would 11 people—one of them a two-year-old child—forsake a perfectly seaworthy ship for a cramped rowboat 100 miles from land?

Suspicion immediately fell upon the captain and crew of the *Dei Gratia.* They were accused of storming the *Mary Celeste* and killing everyone on board so they could grab the ship for the salvage money it would bring. But a court of inquiry could find no evidence of piracy, and the captain was cleared. (He did, in fact, collect the salvage fee, but it was quite small.)

Then it was suggested that the *Dei Gratia*'s owner had conspired with the *Mary Celeste* crew to kill Captain Briggs and his family and sink the ship so he could collect the insurance money. But the crew supposedly botched the job, and everybody wound up getting killed. This theory, however, raised more questions than it tried to answer, so it, too, was tossed.

With so few clues, people had a free-for-all guessing what might have happened on board the *Mary Celeste*. Everything from waterspouts to a stranding on a "ghost island"—a shifting sandbar that forms and reforms— was offered. Some thought that food poisoning might have driven a hallucinating crew to jump overboard. Others pointed to the only hatch found open and suggested that alcohol fumes had blown the cover off. (The *Mary Celeste* was carrying 1,700 barrels of commercial alcohol.) Then the captain, seeing a smoky vapor pour from the hold, feared that the ship was about to catch fire and ordered everyone into the lifeboat. But all we have—and are ever likely to have—are bits and pieces, none of which fit together. So the mystery remains, and this is why the *Mary Celeste* is so beloved by those who believe the Bermuda Triangle is somehow cursed.

>> Natural or Supernatural?

It's certainly true that ships have gone down in these waters, never to be seen again. Planes have vanished without a trace. Fishing boats and pleasure craft have disappeared. But were strange, supernatural forces responsible? Did aliens in secret underwater outposts suck down all these vessels like a family of lizards feeding on juicy summer insects? Not quite.

It is a fact of life that pilots make errors in judgment. They become disoriented in bad weather. Engines fail. Ships run aground. They hit icebergs.

Vincent Gaddis could be considered the creator of the Bermuda Triangle. In his 1965 book, *Invisible Horizons*, Gaddis suggested an explanation for all the Triangle's mysterious vanishings. The U.S. Navy, he wrote, was conducting something called the Philadelphia Experiment, trying to eliminate the earth's magnetic field. The resulting vortex would suck down ships and planes *(left)* in sensitive spots around the world. Guess what the navy thought of Gaddis's theory.

They capsize and sink in fierce, unexpected storms. Explosions happen. Hijackings occur. Crews mutiny. Even in this ultramodern world of ours, pirates still roam the seas. And the seas are vast. They are deep. If a search-and-rescue team is not quickly dispatched, wreckage will sink without a trace. Bodies will be lost forever.

But planes don't just fall out of the sky!

Yes, sadly, they do, and the ocean claims them remarkably fast.

So it seems the haunted sea we all love to fear is more myth than curse, more fake than fact. But some legends just won't sink.

25

DAN'S DARING
DISAPPEARANCE

I was never so scared in my life. The guy was practically sitting right next to me! I remember. He was in 18C. We had just started down the runway, and I was, you know, thinking about how takeoffs and landings are the most dangerous part of the flight. That was weird, now that I think of it.

So, the flight attendant comes down the aisle, checking to make sure everybody's belted in, and the guy hands her a note. He's wearing sunglasses and a dark suit, and he doesn't look menacing or anything. He's just a passenger on his way to Seattle, like the rest of us. Only he isn't.

The note says he's got a bomb and he's going to blow the whole plane to kingdom come if he doesn't get $200,000 in cash and four parachutes when we land.

Well, the flight attendant is cool and doesn't let on, but when we reach Seattle, they give the guy what he wants, and he lets everybody go except the pilot and some of the crew. Then they take off again.

Now, this you won't believe. The guy orders the pilot to fly to Mexico, but long before they get there, he somehow gets the cabin door open, straps on a parachute, and jumps! They're 10,000 feet up, the winds are gusting at 80 knots, and it's freezing, but the guy jumps! With the money!

They never found him.

The Northwest Airlines plane *(facing page)* hijacked by D. B. Cooper sits on the runway in Seattle, Washington, as it is refueled. Cooper seemed ill-equipped to skydive out of a jet in high winds *(below)*.

The Northwest Airlines crew recounts the hijacking at a press conference. Cooper first passed a threatening note to the flight attendant *(above, right)*, then warned her that he was carrying a bomb.

But that was only the beginning, although most people thought it was the end. No one, the federal agents said, could have survived a jump over rugged wilderness terrain in such dreadful weather conditions—especially a guy in a business suit! He had called himself Dan Cooper when he purchased his Northwest Airlines flight ticket in Portland, Oregon, November 24, 1971. Whoever he was, the Federal Bureau of Investigation (FBI) said, he was probably dead now.

But the whole thing was deeply unsettling. Cooper had, in fact, hijacked a Boeing 727 and exited the plane with $200,000 in $20 bills. The stunt was beyond risky. It was downright insane. But Cooper did have a parachute—four of them, in fact—and nobody knew anything about him. Had he ever jumped before? Had he, perhaps, been a paratrooper? Did he have more of a plan than authorities supposed? Was it possible that he could have survived? The FBI squirmed. It was a very creepy thought.

Months became years, and Cooper started to become something of a folk hero to people in the Northwest. They wrote songs about him, celebrating his reckless derring-do and what some thought was his success in eluding the FBI. But not the slightest hint of Dan Cooper—either alive or dead—ever surfaced. Then, in 1980, an eight-year-old boy found a muddy packet of money while walking the banks of the Columbia River near Portland, Oregon.

COOPER CASH

Kids find a lot of interesting stuff when they're out exploring. Cool rocks, arrowheads, watches. Sometimes they even find money—nickels, dimes, and if they're lucky, quarters. But when Brian Ingram found bundles of $20 bills on a muddy riverbank, he knew the money hadn't just fallen out of the sky. Or had it? Brian and his family turned the money over to the police and later learned his find was part of the Cooper payoff. Brian received a $2,760 reward.

29

In February 1980, eight-year-old Brian Ingram found $5,800 along the banks of the Columbia River. Here he shows reporters where he discovered the money—still in bank bundles.

Federal investigators examined the damaged $20 bills found on the banks of the Columbia River. Some thought it indicated that Cooper had first landed at that spot, but others argued that the river current could have carried the money there.

When the money's serial numbers were checked, they were found to match some of those from the bills given to Cooper. But most of the hijack money—along with the wheat-colored bank bag in which it had been placed—was missing. After almost a decade, the plot was finally beginning to thicken.

>> Duane and the Missing Years

In 1995 Duane Weber lay dying in a Pace, Florida, hospital. His wife, Jo, was at his side. They had been married for 17 years, which had been good ones, mostly. Duane had walked into Jo's life in the late 1970s, and Jo had fallen for him, even though Duane had some secrets. But there, on the thick hospital bed with the stiff, white sheets, Duane Weber was about to share one of them.

"Jo," he whispered. "Listen. I'm Dan Cooper."

Jo blinked. "What?" she said. "What do you mean?" She had never heard the name and had no idea what her husband was talking about. Her face was blank.

Weber searched his wife's eyes and then, frustrated, cried out, "Oh, let it die with me!" But it didn't.

Two months after Duane passed away, Jo sold his van. When the new owners were cleaning it out, they came upon a wallet. It contained U.S. Navy discharge papers for bad conduct in Duane's name. But it also contained a Social Security card and a Missouri State Penitentiary release form for someone named John C. Collins. Jo was now very curious.

Some time later, during a conversation with a friend about Duane's mysterious past, Jo mentioned that her husband had admitted injuring his knee in a parachuting accident.

"What!"

"Yes, just before he died, he told me he had jumped out of a plane and hurt his knee."

Jo's friend goggled. Did Jo ever wonder, she asked, if Duane might have been D. B. Cooper?

"Who?"

When D. B. Cooper hijacked an airplane, he committed a federal offense under the Air Piracy Act of 1961 (Cooper's FBI wanted poster is at left). That is, he violated a law enacted by the U.S. Congress. The government does not take air piracy lightly, and hijackers are pursued by the Federal Aviation Administration (FAA), the Department of Defense (DOD), and the FBI. After Cooper escaped, the FBI launched an exhaustive search, including sending Identification Orders (wanted posters) to police agencies across the country. Cooper's hijacking also prompted the FAA to institute a procedure that's become a familiar routine in any airport—the screening of all passengers and carry-on luggage.

"The skyjacker! The guy who jumped out of a plane in the early '70s with a bag of loot and was never found!"

In May 1996, Jo Weber was in the library, poring over a book about the infamous D. B. Cooper. The FBI's composite sketch looked eerily like a younger Duane, and the description matched: 6 feet tall, 170 pounds, black hair, mid-40s, a chain-smoker. And then, Jo remembered, there was that dream. One night, Duane had mumbled something in his sleep about leaving his fingerprints on the aft stairs. He had woken up in a sweat.

Aft stairs? Jo had thought at the time. Like on an airplane?

Jo read on. The wheat-colored canvas bag! She had seen that! It had been in a picnic cooler in Duane's van. And the plane ticket for a flight on Northwest—it had been mixed in with some old tax records.

The whole thing seemed impossible. Whom had she married? D. B. Cooper, Duane Weber, or John Collins? One was dishonorably discharged from the service, one had been in prison, and one was an airline hijacker. And one or all of these men had died in a Florida hospital, known to the people of Pace as a mild-mannered antiques dealer.

If Jo's husband had, indeed, been D. B. Cooper, he had pulled off quite a disappearance. On that night in 1971, he had leaped into infamy and vanished without a trace. He had scared everyone but injured no one. He had gotten away with the money but had spent almost none of it.

It was death that finally found him, and Cooper had no choice but to confess. Death knew his real name.

Prison Break

They said we were the worst of the worst, and that's why we wound up on the Rock. Al Capone was there, and so was Machine Gun Kelly. The Choctaw Kid was in for 99 years plus life. Gangsters, racketeers, murderers, train robbers. Bad guys, all of us. That's what they said.

The place was awful. Foghorns all the time, bellowing in the middle of the night like trapped animals, like us, howling to be set free. And it was damp, cold and damp, and I swear, I never saw so many pelicans. That's how this stink hole got its name. Some Spanish explorer once called it Isla de los

They told us we'd never be able to escape. If the freezing water didn't get us, the sharks would. A few guys tried anyway. They didn't make it. Then came Frank Morris. On the day he arrived, he said he was leaving. He'd be the one. Took him six months to set it up, and then one night he was gone. To this day, nobody knows what happened to him.

Frank had probably drowned, they said. They never found his body, but they couldn't leave it that way. They couldn't have people thinking that somebody might have actually escaped from the escape-proof prison. So a little while later, they shut the place down for good.

I hear they're giving tours these days. Frank would have thought that was funny. Maybe he's laughing right now.

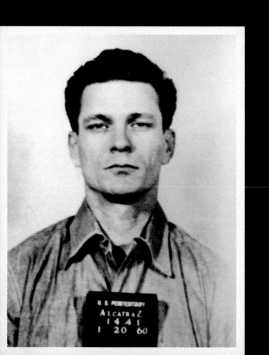

Frank Morris was a bank robber and had served time here and there. But he had a fondness for escaping, so after his last attempt, they sentenced him to 10 years and sent him to Alcatraz.

Alcatraz Penitentiary *(facing page)* was large, cold, and impersonal. It was built to house convicts who had tried to escape other prisons, as Frank Morris *(left)* had.

Morris looked at the cold rock walls and heard the shuffle of dead men's feet. He heard the clang of iron doors meeting locks that couldn't be picked. He smelled the pungent disinfectant. No, he thought, this ain't for me. And by the end of his first day on the Rock, he had already started to plan his escape.

>> The Plan Is Hatched

Alcatraz sits upon a tiny, wind-blown island in San Francisco Bay, a mere one mile from Fishermen's Wharf and the tourists who once paid a nickel to gawk at the famous prison through high-powered telescopes.

Alcatraz sits on an island in the middle of San Francisco Bay. Before it was a prison, Alcatraz was a military post guarding the entrance to the bay.

Guards watched the perimeter (outer edge) of Alcatraz Island from wooden towers. Even if prisoners managed to get past the guards and fences, chances were slim of surviving the water and dangerous currents of the bay.

There were guards, of course, and fences strung with barbed wire. During the day, a prisoner had little chance to get to the water's edge without being seen. But even if he made it, he had no place to go except into the icy waters of San Francisco Bay, where hungry sharks and dangerous currents challenged him to take his best shot. The lights on the shore across the bay shone gaily. The hilly, sun-soaked streets were so tantalizingly close but impossible to reach—if, thought Morris, you were stupid enough to try to swim, which Morris wasn't. He already knew how he was going to get off the island. He just needed to figure a way out of the prison.

Within weeks of his arrival, Morris learned that three years earlier, a fan motor had been removed from an air shaft leading to the roof above his cellblock. The motor had never been replaced. That meant the shaft should be open all the way up to the roof. It was the perfect escape route. But how would Morris get into the shaft? It seemed impossible, unless . . .

Just beneath Morris's sink was an air vent. Beyond the vent, a narrow corridor for water pipes and electric cables ran along the outer wall. If Morris could remove the vent and enlarge the hole so he could crawl into the corridor, he could make his way to the shaft. Then it was up to the roof and gone!

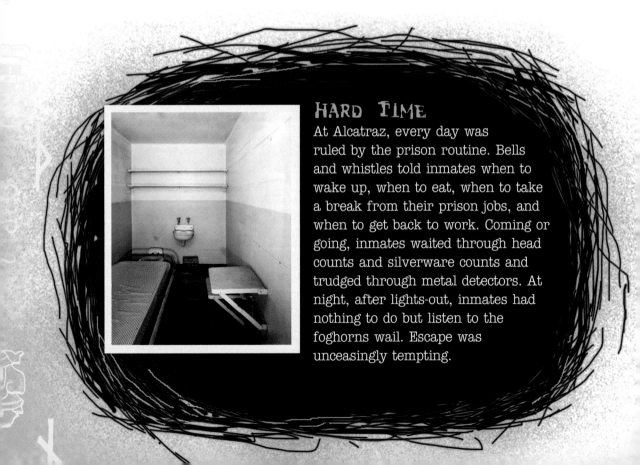

HARD TIME

At Alcatraz, every day was ruled by the prison routine. Bells and whistles told inmates when to wake up, when to eat, when to take a break from their prison jobs, and when to get back to work. Coming or going, inmates waited through head counts and silverware counts and trudged through metal detectors. At night, after lights-out, inmates had nothing to do but listen to the foghorns wail. Escape was unceasingly tempting.

He'd need tools, which were easy enough to steal from the prison workshop. But he'd also have to hide what he was doing. One of the inmates had
an accordion, and that gave him an idea. He could order one for himself,
paying for it with money he'd earned in the workshop. Then he could lean
the accordion against the hole. But as the work progressed and the hole
grew larger, Morris realized he'd have to make a false section of wall. He
also decided that his escape plan—now almost fully hatched—had a bet-
ter chance of succeeding if he had some accomplices.

>> Papier-Mâché Heads and Water Wings

John and Clarence Anglin had turned bank robbing into a
family enterprise. And thanks to the California prison sys-
tem, they were still spending Sunday dinners together.

Clarence Anglin (*left*) and John William Anglin (*right*) were sent to Alcatraz after several attempts to escape from prison in Georgia.

(They were held, of course, in different cells.) Toughened by frequent stays in the state penitentiary, the Anglins would make savvy breakout companions. Morris eagerly recruited them.

They would make their escape in the dead of night, Morris told them, leaving behind papier-mâché heads on their pillows and fake bodies under the covers.

"How do we get across the bay?" the Anglins wanted to know.

"Water wings," Morris told them. "Or maybe a raft. We inflate plastic raincoat sleeves with air. The coats are right there in the basement workshop."

"Hey! We could steal a new one each day!" said Clarence, grinning.

"Yeah! And wear it back to our cells!"

Clearly, the Anglins liked this idea.

"It'll take some time," Morris said.

"We got nothing but," said Clarence.

Morris had served less than a year of his sentence when the digging was complete, the papier-mâché heads were painted and dry, and the way to the roof was clear.

"Let's go," said the Anglins eagerly. "Let's go tonight."

But Morris wanted to wait. "I need to study the currents first," he told them.

"What for?"

"Do you know how cold that water is?"

The Anglins shrugged. It was a detail they didn't think was too important.

"Cold," said Morris. "Cold enough to kill you. You in the mood to fight a current and maybe wind up working against it while the water's freezing your legs off till you can't feel 'em anymore and you can't kick? When you're moving with the current, it takes less time."

So the Anglins agreed to wait. But their patience quickly wore thin, and some time around nine o'clock on the evening of June 11, Morris heard John Anglin's muffled voice on the other side of the fake wall.

"We're going," he hissed.

"No," Morris whispered back. It was a week before the agreed-upon date. "Yes. Now," said Anglin, and a moment later he was working his way along the utility corridor toward the air shaft.

The Morris-Anglin Escape Route

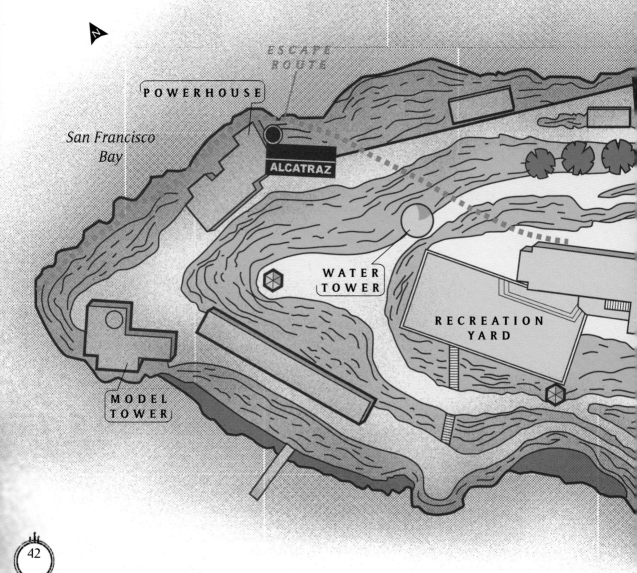

Soon after lights-out at 9:30 on the night of June 11, 1962, Morris and the Anglins began their escape. They crawled out of their cells through the tunnels they had spent months digging. They then made their way down a utility corridor and climbed up a shaft to the cell house roof. Dodging the sweeping beams of the prison searchlights, they ran across the rooftop and

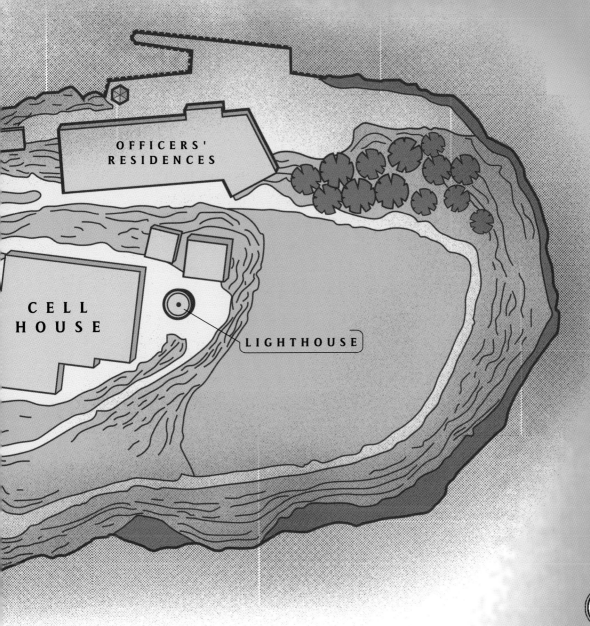

OFFICERS'
RESIDENCES

CELL
HOUSE

LIGHTHOUSE

climbed down some pipes along an exterior wall. Once on the ground, they ran for the shelter of the powerhouse, a large building housing the prison's generators. From there, the three escapees climbed over two fences and headed for the water's edge.

Morris had no choice. When the lights were turned off for the night, he set the papier-mâché head on his pillow, shaped the blankets into a vague human form, and crawled into the utility corridor. Within minutes he had joined John and Clarence Anglin on the roof of the prison. Dodging the powerful beacons atop the guardhouses, the three slipped to the ground. The entire island was bathed by floodlights. Searching out the few shadows, the men moved to the inner chain-link fence, scaled it, and then tackled the barbed wire fence that marked the outer perimeter. Stealthily, they crept to the water's edge, inflated their makeshift water wings, and entered the icy, black waters of San Francisco Bay.

>> Gone!

Nobody knew there had been a prison break until the following morning. By then Morris and the Anglins were either lying at the bottom of San Francisco Bay or had disappeared in the crowded city they had remarkably managed to reach.

The police, the Coast Guard, and prison officials searched the water, of course, but all they found was a plastic bag with some family photographs, a few addresses, and a receipt made out to Clarence Anglin. It was a tantalizing piece of evidence that meant absolutely nothing.

The bay had been calm and the currents in their favor, but no one ever reported seeing the men whose daring escape closed Alcatraz. Had the freezing waters numbed them and pulled them under, one by one? Had they been killed in a shoot-out somewhere, their fingers clutching bank sacks filled with hastily stolen bills? Or did they all laugh softly from a back booth in a backwater diner when they learned that National Park Service rangers had started giving tours of the prison you couldn't get out of?

Whatever the outcome, it was quite a disappearance.

No Escape

Thirty-six prisoners took their best shot at getting off the Rock ahead of schedule. In 1941 John Bayless made it to the shoreline, waded into the icy water, and immediately gave up. Theodore Cole and Ralph Roe slipped into the bay during a fierce storm and were officially classified as drowned. Others were shot by officers or recaptured. Only Frank Morris and the Anglin brothers leave us wondering. . . .

PRISON BREAK

45

>> Find Out More

Books// Klingel, Cynthia. *Amelia Earhart: Aviation Pioneer.* Chanhassen, MN: The Child's World, 2003.
This biography of the famous aviator features historical photographs.

Oxlade, Chris. *The Mystery of the Bermuda Triangle.* Portsmouth, NH: Heinemann Library, 2001.
This book offers scientific explanations and natural causes for the disappearances of ships and planes in the Bermuda Triangle.

Websites// Alcatraz History
http://www.alcatrazhistory.com
This history of the island penitentiary features a diagram of the island and cell house, biographies of famous inmates, details of escape attempts, and a mini-photo tour.

The Earhart Project
http://www.tighar.org/Projects/Earhart/AEdescr.html
TIGHAR's website features photographs, maps, news stories, and myths about Earhart's disappearance and the continuing search for clues to this mystery.

The Un-Mystery of the Bermuda Triangle
http://www.unmuseum.org/triangle.htm
The Unmuseum presents its argument for debunking the supernatural aspect of the Bermuda Triangle. The website includes a brief history of Bermuda Triangle lore.

Movies// "Ghost Ships." *History's Mysteries.* New York: A&E Home Video, 2001. Not rated.
This episode of *History's Mysteries* looks at the *Mary Celeste* and other mysterious vessels found on the high seas.

The Mysteries of Amelia Earhart. New York: A&E Home Video, 2000. Not rated.
Amelia Earhart's rise to fame as an aviator and her last flight are examined in this documentary.

The Pursuit of D. B. Cooper. Beverly Hills, CA: Polygram Filmed Entertainment, 1981. Rated PG.
Starring Treat Williams and Robert Duvall, this movie guesses at how D. B. Cooper may have survived his jump and escaped to a new life.

>> About the Author

Born in Baltimore, Maryland, Judith Herbst grew up in Queens, New York, where she learned to jump double Dutch with amazing skill. She has since lost that ability. A former English teacher, she ran away from school in her tenure year to become a writer. Her first book for kids was *Sky Above and Worlds Beyond,* whose title, she admits, was much too long. She loves to write and would rather be published, she says, than be rich, which has turned out to be the case. Herbst spends summers in Maine on a lake with her cats and laptop.

>> Photo Acknowledgments

Photographs and illustrations in this book are used by permission of: Bill Hauser, pp. 4–5, 10–11, 12, 20, 22–23, 27, 31, 39, 42–43, 44–45; © Brown Brothers, p. 6; © Stuart Klipper, p. 7; © Bettmann/CORBIS, pp. 8, 14, 16, 26, 28, 29, 30, 35, 40; © Hulton|Archive by Getty Images, pp. 11, 22; © CORBIS, p. 13; © Reuters/CORBIS, p. 15; Knights of Columbus Headquarters Museum, p. 17; © Fortean Picture Library, pp. 19, 25; © Time Life Pictures/Getty Images, p. 32; courtesy of the Library of Congress, pp. 34 (HABS, CAL,38-ALCA,1-A-20), 36 (HABS, CAL,38-ALCA,1-1), 37 (HABS, CAL,38-ALCA,1-I-1), 38 (HABS, CAL,38-ALCA,1-A-23).

Cover image by © Bettmann/CORBIS.

48